J. H. YOUNG

Bubble Tea: 10 Places to Visit in Boston

First edition

This book was professionally typeset on Reedsy.
Find out more at reedsy.com

Contents

1

Introduction

Welcome to the city of Boston! Whether you are a local, college student, transplant, or tourist, I hope this guide will be useful to you. As both a local and bubble tea addict, I wanted to create a guide in order to share some of my favorite bubble tea shops with friends and families as they explore the city.

Boston is a city steeped in history. First, it is the largest and most populated city in the New England area. Historically, the region was long inhabited by the Native American tribes of Massachusetts. It wasn't until 1630 when a group of Puritans, led by John Winthrop, sailed across the sea and colonized the area. The Puritans named the area Boston after the same English town in which many Puritans immigrated from.

From then on, Boston has been the site of many historical events and achievements. During the 1630s, the first and oldest public school, Boston Latin School, was established where notable individuals such as Benjamin Franklin, John Hancock, and Samuel Adams attended. The school is still running and remains the highest performing institution within the Boston Public School system. In addition, and although technically NOT in Boston, Harvard University was established in Cambridge. Still, it draws many anticipating high school seniors, college students, and tourists from around the world to Boston in order to visit this prestigious institution.

Later, the city became the site of many historical events including the Boston Massacre, Boston Tea Party, and the Boston Bombing. It is the location of the Old State House, which is where many decisions were made during the American Revolution, and Paul Revere's house, who is known for his midnight ride.

Today, the city continues to play a pivotal location for individuals worldwide. It is the leader of many prestigious educational institutions, medical and scientific practices, and research centers. The city's landscape and population have changed throughout the years, however it continues to draw a diversified crowd seeking new opportunities and experiences.

If you're a bubble tea addict like me, you'll probably want to know where you can fulfill your bubble tea cravings. Bubble tea, also known as Boba tea, is becoming a popular drink sought out by both locals and tourists. Although it feels like a relatively new trend, it has always been popular in Asian countries and communities. It originated in Taiwan during the early 1980s and is known for its tapioca pearls, variety of colors, and flavors. Today you can find both tea-based and non-tea based drinks.

This guide is for entertainment purposes, and is in no way a rating system for the bubble tea shops listed. I highly recommend visiting all businesses as they are unique in their own way.

Enjoy,

J. H. Young

2

Matcha Cafe Maiko

I f you are planning a visit to Boston or moving here for the first time, you've probably already looked up "things to do in Boston." The Fenway area is one of the most popular destinations. Fenway is famous for Fenway Park which is the oldest stadium in Major League Baseball and where the Red Sox call home. Although primarily known for its stadium, the Fenway area is also home to many institutions. Colleges such as Simmons University, parts of Boston University, and parts of Northeastern crossover into the Fenway area. Fenway also includes Longwood, which is the location of world-renowned medical research centers and hospitals.

If you happen to be in Fenway and are walking down Boylston Street, Matcha Cafe Maiko is very close by. First opened in Hawaii, Matcha Cafe Maiko is a franchise which prides itself in using authentic matcha powder directly sourced from Harima Garden, Japan. Harima Garden is located in Uji which is known for sourcing high quality matcha. The cafe's mission is to provide its customers with authentic and high quality matcha tea drinks.

You'll find Boston's Matcha Cafe Maiko at the intersection of Queensberry Street and Jersey Street. When you pass through the doors, you'll be instantly hit by the powerful aroma of premium Japanese matcha. They have a great selection of products including hochija, which is another type of Japanese green tea that gives off a sweet nutty and smokey flavor. The menu also includes several soft-serve ice cream flavors which can be eaten in a cone or included in a float. So if you love matcha, like I do, then you should definitely stop by Matcha Cafe Maiko.

Location(s):

Matcha Cafe Maiko
   115 Jersey Street
   Boston, MA 02215

Kokuto Matcha Latte Float

3

Shinmio Tea

Not too far from Fenway lies Beacon Street where Shinmio Tea can be found. Originally laid out during the 1850s, Beacon Street was designed as a dam that extended over the Charles River Basin and to provide access to Boston for residents living in Brookline. In 1888 the first railroad tracks were laid out along the entire street which is now known as the Green Line C branch.

If you are not traveling with a car, don't worry. Boston's public transportation system, or the Massachusetts Bay Transportation Authority (MBTA), is fairly easy to understand. If you are asking locals for directions, they'll probably refer to the MBTA as "the T." It's the same thing. After hopping on the Green Line C branch, get off at Saint Mary's Street which is the closest stop to Shinmio Tea.

Shinmio Tea is a small establishment, so it might be easy to miss. Once inside, you'll immediately notice the large glowing logo of a cat with a mermaid tail against the wall. Like I mentioned before, it's a small place, so there isn't really any space to sit down. Nevertheless, you do have the entirety of Beacon Street to explore while sipping some sweet tasting bubble tea.

Shinmio Tea's mission is to provide their customers with the best tea experience. They claim to only use premium tea leaves, organic milk, and fresh fruits. In addition, Shinmio Tea is unique in that it keeps to a small menu and rotates seasonal specials. So, if you are in Boston during different seasons, Shinmio Tea will have a new drink for you. This store is on the pricier side for bubble tea, but this is the company's only store and definitely worth trying.

Top Favorite Drinks:

- Fresh Strawberry Milk w. Boba
- Osmanthus Oolong w. Boba
- Very Black Grapes SmooTea
- Jasmine Green w. Boba
- Very Strawberry SmooTea

Location(s):

Shinmio Tea
900 Beacon St Unit D
Boston, MA 02215

4

Tiger Sugar

After exploring Brookline, you might find yourself on the north side of Harvard Avenue. Harvard Avenue is a long commercial strip that is well visited by college students, locals, tourists, and food enthusiasts. The avenue was first established in the 1630s as part of a highway connection between Boston and Harvard Square. Later, during the 1910s and 1920s, Harvard Avenue became an upscale residential location. Today, Harvard Avenue continues to be a vital commercial strip lined with mostly restaurants and small stores. If you are taking public transportation, take the Green Line B branch and hop off the Harvard Avenue stop. This area has several bubble tea stores, but I am only going to mention three.

Walking north along Harvard Avenue, and to your left hand side, is one of many bubble tea shops. This specific store is really small and can be easily missed if you're not paying attention. You'll have to go down a small step of stairs and, once inside, there is no room to sit down so you'll most likely be leaving right away.

Founded in 2017 in Taichung Taiwan, Tiger Sugar is a franchise specializing in brown sugar boba, so if you love brown sugar anything, this might be the spot for you.

After spending hours of research and trial and error, the founders of Tiger Sugar perfected the original "drink dessert." By mixing caramelized brown sugar syrup and fresh milk, it creates a creamy and unique image that can be compared to the stripes of a tiger, hence the name. Since then, the company has gone international and is credited for popularizing the brown sugar boba drink. In the United States, Tiger Sugar can only be found in Boston, New York, and Los Angeles so far. So, if you haven't tried it already, be sure to check this off your list.

Top Favorite Drinks:

- Brave as a Tiger
- Tiger Jelly
- Tiger Meets Chocolate
- Tiger Meets Coffee
- Tiger Meets Pudding

Location(s):

Tiger Sugar (Allston)
  181 Harvard Ave
  Allston, MA 02134

Tiger Sugar (Chinatown)
  14 Tyler Street
  Boston, MA 02111

5

Gong Cha

I f you are still on Harvard Avenue, continue walking north, but this time paying attention to your right hand side. It is no more than a 2 minute walk away. Our next stop is Gong Cha, and I highly recommend this specific store because it also houses Mochinut, a company that specializes in mochi donuts.

Gong Cha is another franchise that has successfully launched across the world. They are one of the better known bubble tea shops, so you may be already familiar with it.

In 1996 Kaohsiung, Taiwan, two friends, Huang and Wu, worked together to establish their very first tea shop. They decided to name it "Gong Cha," a phrase used when offering the highest quality of teas to the emperor. It roughly translates to "tribute to the emperor" and symbolizes a great act of honoring the emperor.

Like paying tribute to the emperor, Huang and Wu hoped to do the same for their customers. They dedicated themselves to only using the best ingredients and creating high quality recipes. This small establishment started becoming popular and drew in more customers. Eventually, the news spread to the rest of Taiwan. However, it wasn't until 2006 when the duo officially branded Gong Cha as a franchise and started opening stores around the world. Their official philosophy is "To inspire the human spirit and create happiness." So, while you are enjoying some Gong Cha tea, I hope it'll bring some joy to your day.

Since Gong Cha is a well known franchise, it actually has several establishments in Massachusetts. However, I am only going to be listing the locations that are IN Boston.

Location(s):

Gong Cha (Allston)
  154 Harvard Ave
  Allston, MA 02134

Gong Cha (Chinatown)
  40-44 Harrison Ave
  Boston, MA 02111

Gong Cha (Newbury Street)
  270 Newbury Street
  Boston, MA 02116

Gong Cha (Northeastern University)
  281 Huntington Ave
  Boston, MA 02115

Gong Cha (Dorchester)
  1460 Dorchester Ave
  Space C
  Dorchester, MA 02122

6

Kung Fu Tea

My third Harvard Ave recommendation is just across the street. It is another successful and widely known franchise: Kung Fu Tea. The company claims to be America's number one bubble tea franchise, so you may have already had Kung Fu Tea before. If so, feel free to skip this recommendation.

In 2009, after returning from a trip to Taiwan, Allen Wang and his two friends, Michael and Ray, were exploring the streets of Flushing Queens. The trio reminisced about their time growing up in Taiwan and drinking their favorite bubble tea. They found a local tea store, but the quality of the tea was not the same as they remembered growing up. Then and there the three friends decided to create their own tea business. They called their friend Sean, a successful tea master in Taiwan, to join the team and together sprung the idea of bringing quality tea to America.

The first store opened in 2010 Queens, New York. One of Kung Fu's values is continuous self-improvement. Like learning to master Kung Fu, it takes a lot of practice and self discipline. The founders wanted to embody the same principles when it came to perfecting their own innovative teas.

I am specifically recommending the Allston location as I believe they consistently make quality teas. In addition, they also have several tables and seats, so you and your friends and family can sit down and relax.

There are a ton of Kung Fu Tea locations, so if you can't make it to the Allston location, there are a ton of other locations in Boston as well.

The Massachusetts Top 10 Drinks:

- Kung Fu Milk Tea
- Kung Fu Milk Green Tea
- Kung Fu Oolong Milk Tea
- Mango Green Tea
- Coconut Milk Tea
- Taro Milk Tea
- Cocoa Cream Wow
- Thai Milk Tea
- Mango Slush
- Passionfruit Green Tea

Location(s):

Kung Fu Tea (Chinatown)
66 Kneeland Street
Boston, MA 02111

Kung Fu Tea (Symphony)
334 Massachusetts Ave
Boston, MA 02115

Kung Fu Tea (Packards Corner)
1 Brighton Ave
Allston, MA 02134

Kung Fu Tea (Allston)
131 Harvard Ave
Allston, MA 02134

Kung Fu Tea (Cleveland Circle)
  1916 Beacon Street
  Brighton, MA 02135

7

LimeRed Teahouse

Not far from Harvard Ave lies Commonwealth Avenue. Boston University lines along a majority of Commonwealth Ave, however if you are heading towards the west end where it intersects with Allston, there is another sweet bubble tea spot: LimeRed Tea House. It is near Hong Kong Supermarket, a Chinese supermarket that has sustained many locals. If you are taking public transportation, you can take the Green Line B branch and hop off at Packards Corner.

LimeRed's mission is to refresh the traditional Taiwanese drink with their full espresso bar. The company uses classic Brazilian coffee beans, fresh milk from local farms, and coffee flavors such as Caramel Macchiato. What you get in the end is caffeinated bubble tea! This location is great for college students who need to crunch out a paper or do some studying. There are plenty of tables and seats so you'll see at least one of two individuals working there as well.

LimeRed TeaHouse also serves a variety of baked goods including french macrons, butter mochi cakes, and more. Their different locations serve additional treats, but the Boston location also serves cheesecake, earl gray shortbread cookies, green tea matcha sugar cookies, and croissants. This is the only location in Boston, so be sure to visit!

Top Favorite Drinks:

- Assam Black Milk Tea
- Jasmine Milk Tea
- Thai Milk Tea

Location(s):

LimeRed Tea House
 1092 Commonwealth Ave
 Boston, MA 02215

8

Newbury Street

Newbury Street is another top destination for visitors.

Originally submerged underwater, the Back Bay area did not have land until the mid-1850s. In order to build additional buildings and housing, landscapers began to fill the harbor with dirt into what we now know as the Back bay area. Today, the neighborhood includes several architectural landmarks including the Old South Church, the first Boston Public Library, and John Hancock Tower.

During the 1880s and 1890s, with more individuals settling in Boston, the city decided Newbury Street would become a residential neighborhood. Apartment buildings were slowly constructed simultaneously as landscapers continued to fill in the harbor. It took over forty years for the land to completely fill to the entire harbor. Today, if you are walking down the street, take a closer look at the architecture of the buildings. You may notice that the architectural style changes the further you walk down the street. The slight style changes reflect the styles popular at the time they were built.

Newbury Street attracted many of Boston's elite and was considered the most desirable place to live. It wasn't until the early 1900s when the first commercial store opened for business. Fashion and apparel stores were popular during the roaring twenties, so retailers began taking up residency on the first floors. In order to draw in more customers, business owners began placing large glass windows to display their luxury goods. Today, Newbury Street continues to be known for its high end shops, but now includes a multitude of restaurants, cafes, and dessert spots. In addition to all the establishments that line along Newbury Street, the brownstone buildings and cobbled sidewalks are what really attracts visitors as a reminder of colonial New England.

I will be recommending two bubble tea shops along this famous destination.

9

Ten One Tea House

O n the corner of Newbury Street and Gloucester Street resides Ten One Tea House.

Founded in 2019, the founders named their store TEN, like having a score of 10 out of 10, and ONE because they strive to be the best handcrafted teas. Ten One Tea House strives to make high quality teas, and therefore are selective with their partnerships. They emphasize on their use of organic dried flowers, fruits, and premium loose-leaf tea in order to create healthy drinks for their customers. In addition, they also serve some unique shaped desserts.

In my opinion, Tea One House has one of the most aesthetically pleasing teas. From classic milk teas to flavorful fruit teas, the shop offers a wide selection. My personal favorites are Drifting in Dreams, a dark bluish green drink reminiscent of a foggy day, and Lavender Forest, a purplish pink drink that'll lift your spirits. The company only has four stores in total with two in Boston, one in Somerville, Massachusetts, and another in Providence. So, if you are in the area, this is definitely a place worth trying.

Location(s):

Ten One Teahouse (Newbury)
  279 Newbury Street
  Boston, MA

Ten One Teahouse (Fenway)
  1323 Boylston Street
  Boston, MA

10

Yi Fang Taiwan Fruit Tea

Not too far from Ten One Tea House is another great tea shop: Yi Fang Taiwan Fruit Tea. It is a franchise famous for, as the name suggests, their fruit teas. The company's founder named the franchise after their grandmother, Yi Fang. In Taiwan, Yi Fang married a farmer who carried on his family's legacy of cultivating pineapples. He worked tirelessly everyday in the scorching sun. Worried for her husband's health, Yi Fang used the overripe pineapples to create preservable pineapple jam and drinks for her husband to enjoy. Like the authenticity and sincere love shown between Yi Fang and her husband, the company's mission is to spread the same love to their customers. Yi Fang also emphasizes their use of homemade organic cane sugar, seasonal fresh fruits, and natural ingredients, so they do not use any concentrated juice, powders, or syrups.

Like many other stores on Newbury Street, this establishment is quite small. So, you won't be lingering here for too long. Before you go make sure to also try their egg pancakes. As of now they have four flavored fillings: the signature, custard, taro, and pearl milk tea.

Top 10 Favorite Drinks

- Taro With Milk
- Green Pum Green Tea
- Matcha Tea Latte
- Yi Fang Fruit Tea
- Oolong Tea Latte
- Winter Melon Latte
- Brown Sugar Pearl Oolong Tea Latte
- Mango Pomelo Sago
- Brown Sugar Pearl Matcha Latte
- Passion Fruit Green Tea

Location(s):

Yi Fang Taiwan Fruit Tea
   215 Newbury Street
   1st Floor
   Boston, MA 02116

11

Chinatown

I f there is a local Chinatown then there is most definitely a bubble tea shop. My last two recommendations are in Boston's very own Chinatown near Downtown Boston.

As mentioned before, Boston is steeped in history and its Chinatown is no exception. Historically, Boston's Chinatown is the only Chinatown in all of New England. In 1870, the owners of Sampson's Shoe Factory in North Adams, Massachusetts hired Chinese laborers from California to work as strikebreakers. They noticed that these laborers were willing to work for lower wages and yet, still provide better services than previous laborers. After finishing their work with the shoe factory, some Chinese laborers returned to California while others stayed due to the rising riots and hate crimes in California.

Boston's Chinese population during this time consisted mostly of men. This is because many Chinese immigrants came to the United States with the intention of returning back home to China. Seeking opportunities, most men were trying to earn enough money to improve their economic situation(s) for them and their families. These immigrants worked hard and often lonely lives due to the increasing anti-immigration backlash.

Boston's Chinese immigrants settled themselves between Downtown and the South End. This area was built on landfill intended for railroads and row houses, thus making it undesirable and cheap. This area was associated with low property value and low rent housing. The Chinese were able to establish a small community which helped provide a sense of belonging and home.

The influx of Chinese immigrants slowed after the passing of the Chinese Exclusion Act of 1882, which made it illegal for any Chinese immigrant from entering the country and banned the naturalization of Chinese people already living in the United States. It wasn't until 1943, when the Exclusion Act was repealed, when the Chinese American population began to grow and change to what we see today.

12

TeaDo

Chinatown has many amazing and authentic Chinese restaurants, and that includes their bubble tea shops. On Tyler Street you'll find Boston's Tea Do, a contemporary tea house that provides a wide selection of drinks and delicious food. Tea Do's mission is to create bubble tea experiences that will satisfy customers' cravings and to provide a drink that'll fit whatever kind of mood you are in. They offer a variety of tea drinks from traditional milk teas to fresh fruit teas.

In addition, TeaDo serves delicious onigiri and takoyaki which is great when you are craving a late night snack. TeaDo is very popular among locals, so be sure to try it because the company is only established in a handful of states.

Top Favorite Drinks:

- Brown Sugar Tiger Milk
- Tiger Milk Tea

- Mango Smoothie
- Thai Milk Tea
- Avocado Smoothie
- Taro Milk Tea
- Zen's Awakening

Location(s):
TeaDo
8 Tyler Street
Boston, MA 02111

13

Cafe Darq

L ast on my list is Chinatown's newest bubble tea shop: Cafe Darq. Located on Beach Street, Cafe Darq claims to be an Asian-style bubble tea shop with a European-style interior. They are dedicated to providing premium specialty teas, coffee, and artisan treats.

Cafe Darq definitely has a very different vibe and atmosphere compared to other cafes in Boston. Lined along the windows, there are plenty of bar stool seats to sit down as well as a couple of tables. Cafe Darq hopes to make customers feel welcomed and cozy while also feeling high class.

Cafe Darq really promotes their selection of Belgium and Leonidas chocolates, and its really their top selling product. However, Cafe Darq is unique in that they use products from Mem Tea, a tea shop in Cambridge, and George Howell Coffee, a great coffee brand.

This Boston location seems to be the company's first and only store so far, so be sure to visit before leaving Boston!

Location(s):

Cafe Darq
  40 Beach Street
  Boston, MA 02111

14

Conclusion

T hank you for picking up this book and taking the time to read it. Again, these are not reviews and are my personal preferences. I hope you enjoyed this book and that it helps you plan your next trip to Boston, your next outing with friends, or just getting your bubble tea fix.

If you found this book to be helpful, I would really appreciate it if you left a favorable review on Amazon!

Again, thank you!

Resources

Blumenthal, R. L. (2021, May 12). *Tiger Sugar Boba Chain Expands to Boston's Chinatown*. Eater Boston. Retrieved August 5, 2022, from https://boston.eater.com/2021/5/12/22432793/tiger-sugar-boba-chain-expands boston-chinatown

Boston - The contemporary city. (n.d.). Encyclopedia Britannica. Retrieved August 5, 2022, from https://www.britannica.com/place/Bost on/The-contemporary-city

Boston National Historical Park. (n.d.). *An Early History of Boston's Chinatown (U.S. National Park Service)*. National Park Service. Retrieved August 5, 2022, from https://www.nps.gov/articles/000/boston-chin atown.htm

Brookline Preservation Commission. (n.d.). *History of Beacon St*. Brookline Historical Society. Retrieved August 5, 2022, from https://b rooklinehistoricalsociety.org/history/presComm/beaconSt.asp

History of Newbury Street Real Estate. (n.d.). Back Bay Apartments. http://backbayapartments.com/articles/2017/October/History-of-Newbury-Street-Real-Estate.php

History.com Editors. (2019, March 13). *Boston: A City Steeped in U.S. History*. HISTORY. Retrieved August 5, 2022, from https://www.histo

ry.com/topics/us-states/boston-massachusetts

Krishna, P. (2017, June 6). *A Brief History of Boba.* Food & Wine. Retrieved August 5, 2022, from https://www.foodandwine.com/tea/ bubble-tea-taiwanese-street-drink-turned-american-addiction

Old Town Trolley Tours. (2022, June 16). *Newbury Street Things To Do and Information Guide.* Retrieved August 5, 2022, from https://www.tr olleytours.com/boston/newbury-street

Made in the USA
Middletown, DE
25 August 2022

72273796R00022